THE Phillie Phanatic's HAPPIEST MEMORIES

By Tom Burgoyne
Illustrated by Len Epstein

Middle Atlantic Press

To Andrew, Daniel, and Matthew
—T.B.

To Alison and Jessie
—L.E.

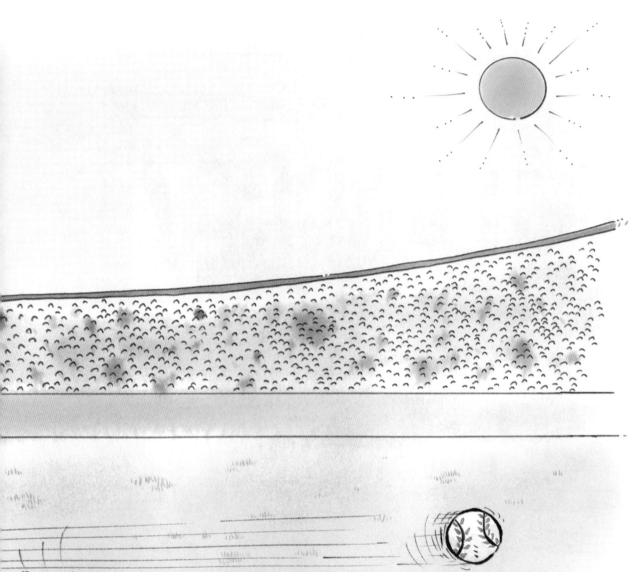

For as long as anyone can remember, the Phillie Phanatic has been the Phillies' number one fan. He leads the crowd in cheers for the home team. He drives his red ATV on the field and sometimes dances with the players, coaches, and umpires. He loves baseball and he loves the Phillies.

One day, high atop Veterans Stadium in his room behind the big video screen, the Phillie Phanatic was sorting his baseball cards.

His mother, Phoebe Phanatic, walked into his room and took a look around.
The Phanatic's room was a mess. "Phanatic, I want you to clean your
room this instant," she demanded.

"But Mom, I cleaned my room last week," the Phanatic pleaded.
"Then why does it look like a hurricane just came through your room?" she asked.
"I don't know," the Phanatic said. "Maybe it's because I like to collect souvenirs
at the baseball games and I never know what to do with them all."

"Oh, Phanatic, you and your souvenirs. Why is it that you collect so much stuff?"
Phoebe asked, "Because Mom, every souvenir brings back a special memory,"
the Phanatic answered. "Like these baseball cards. They are all cards of some of
my favorite baseball players."

"Do you remember this baseball?" the Phanatic asked, showing off one of his prized possessions. "This baseball was used when the Phillies won the World Series."

The Phanatic then pointed to an oversized baseball jersey hanging up in the corner.
"And this was the Phillies jersey I wore at my first Phillies game.
Do you remember that day, Mom?" the Phanatic asked.
"I certainly do," Phoebe replied, starting to understand. "Come with me, Phanatic."

Phoebe took the Phanatic to her bedroom. It was neat and tidy and everything was in its place. "Mom, how come your room is so neat all the time? Don't you collect things to remind you of your special memories?" the Phanatic asked.

Phoebe walked over to the nightstand beside her bed and pulled out a huge photo album from the drawer. "I call this 'My Happiest Memories Book,'" Phoebe said. "All of my happiest memories are inside this book. Would you like to look through it with me, Phanatic?" Phoebe asked.

"I sure would!" the Phanatic exclaimed. Phoebe and the Phillie Phanatic sat down and opened the big photo album.

"GALAPAGOS ISLANDS"

"This is a picture of the Galapagos Islands. It is where you were born. And I took this picture when you were just a baby," Phoebe said.

"BABY PICTURE"

"Wow, Mom, look how small I was," the Phanatic said, marveling at a picture of baby Phanatic.

There was a picture of *Veterans Stadium* when it first opened. It looked different back then. There were yellow and orange seats instead of blue seats. There were two gigantic scoreboards in the outfield and a fountain behind the outfield fence that was called the Dancing Waters.

PHIL and PHILLIS

They even had different mascots back then called Philadelphia Phil and Philadelphia Phillis.

RUNNING THE BASES

"I remember when that picture was taken," the Phanatic said pointing at the next picture. "That was *my* first Phillies game ever! The crowd laughed when I ran around the bases, knocking over the ground crew guys on the field."

"They loved it when I danced on the dugout, too."

The Phanatic pointed at another series of pictures. "That's when the Phillies won the World Series. I got to lead a huge parade down Broad Street after the Phillies won. There must have been over a million people at the parade that day."

WORLD CHAMPIONSHIP RING

"I even got a World Championship ring!"

Phoebe and the Phanatic flipped through the pages of the big photo album.
There were pictures of great players who played at the Vet.

HARRY AND WHITEY

THE "ZAMBONI" MACHINE

There were photos of all the friends the Phanatic had made over the years.

4:00 am

On one page, there was a picture of the Phanatic on top of the dugout in his red pajamas. "Mom, do you remember the time you let me stay up until after 4:00 in the morning to watch the Phillies play?"
"I remember you slept until lunch time the next day," Phoebe chuckled.

There was a picture of the Phanatic launching hot dogs into the crowd and another picture of him shooting t-shirts from his t-shirt launcher.

FANS

Everywhere throughout the book there were pictures of all the great fans the Phanatic has met over the years at Phillies games at the Vet.

When they turned to the last page in the photo album, the page was empty. "Mom, how come there is no picture on the last page?" the Phanatic asked. "I've been so busy, Phanatic, that I haven't gotten a chance to finish putting all the pictures in the book," Phoebe replied.

Just then, the Phanatic had an idea. He ran back into his room to find a picture he had taken of his room the week before, after he had just cleaned it.

"MY CLEAN ROOM"

"Mom, here's a picture of your 'happiest memory' of all," the Phanatic exclaimed.